CANVA DESIGN
FOR *Beginners*

By

Tech Savvy

Thank you for taking the bold step to learn and master canva design using this comprehensive guide.

You will learn faster as this book was written with beginners in mind. Make sure to apply what you learn for positive result. Happy reading…

Disclaimer Notice

The information contained herein is not intended to infringe, create or claim ownership of the app, software or tool of discussion. The app builder or product owner still holds full rights to their product as this guide is strictly for educational purpose. We do not claim any copyright or trademark ownership of any kind. Any views expressed are those of the Author, and do not necessarily reflect the views of any other person, organization or entity.

Table of Contents

Introduction to Canva

Canva is a popular graphic design platform that empowers users to create professional-looking designs without extensive graphic design experience. With its user-friendly interface, vast template library, and robust features, Canva has become a go-to tool for individuals, businesses, and organizations seeking to elevate their visual communication.

Deeper Explanation of Canva

Canva is a cloud-based graphic design platform that provides a wide range of design tools, templates, and resources. Founded in 2012, Canva has revolutionized the way people design, enabling anyone to create stunning graphics, documents, and marketing materials.

Key Features of Canva:

Drag-and-Drop Editor: Intuitive interface for effortless design creation

Huge Template Library: Thousands of pre-designed templates for various design types

Customizable Elements: Extensive collection of fonts, shapes, icons, and graphics

Collaboration Tools: Real-time collaboration and commenting features

Design Assets: Access to millions of images, illustrations, and videos

Typography: Professional typography tools and font library

Color Palette: Advanced color palette generator and management

Image Editing: Built-in image editing and filtering tools

Export Options: Versatile export options for various file formats and resolutions

Integration: Seamless integration with popular platforms and tools

What Can You Create with Canva?

Social Media Graphics: Engaging social media posts, banners, and ads

Presentations: Professional presentations, slides, and decks

Infographics: Informative and visually appealing infographics

Posters: Eye-catching posters, flyers, and brochures

Logos: Custom logos and branding materials

Business Cards: Professional business cards and stationery

Websites: Simple websites and landing pages

Email Newsletters: Attractive email newsletters and campaigns

Magazines: Digital magazines and publications

Branding Materials: Consistent branding materials and guidelines

Benefits of Using Canva

Ease of Use: User-friendly interface for non-designers and designers alike.

Time-Saving: Quick design creation and iteration.

Cost-Effective: Affordable subscription plans and free resources.

Scalability: Suitable for individuals, small businesses, and large enterprises.

Collaboration: Streamlined collaboration and feedback processes.

Consistency: Ensures brand consistency across all designs.

Creativity: Unlocks creativity and inspiration with its vast resources.

Flexibility: Adaptable designs for various formats and resolutions.

Support: Excellent customer support and resources.

Constant Improvement: Regular updates with new features and enhancements.

Getting Started with Canva

Sign Up: Create a free account on (link unavailable).

Explore: Familiarize yourself with the dashboard and features.

Choose a Template: Select a template or start from scratch.

Design: Use the drag-and-drop editor to create your design

Customize: Tailor your design with fonts, colors, and elements

Collaborate: Invite team members or clients to edit and comment

Export: Download or share your design in various formats

Canva is an exceptional graphic design platform that democratizes design, making it accessible to everyone. With its intuitive interface, vast resources, and robust features, Canva empowers users to create stunning designs that elevate their visual communication.

Whether you're a seasoned designer or a beginner, Canva is an excellent tool to explore and master.

Keep in Mind

Canva is a free graphic design platform, perfect for those who want to create beautifully designed items for their business, but do not have extensive design experience. The user-friendly drag and drop platform allows anyone to create social media posts, logos, flyers, presentations, videos, and more.

Here's how small businesses can optimize Canva to promote their business

If you have no design background, don't be discouraged. Canva is helpful no matter your experience level. Canva's in-depth tutorial platform will teach you all you need to know! The platform's tutorials include everything from how to choose the right font, creating a consistent brand, and designing a branded presentation. No matter the design question you may have, Canva has tutorials to help novices hone their skills and successfully create marketing materials for their business.

In addition to the tutorials that will help you get started, Canva has in-depth courses to help users sharpen their skills. Courses include social media mastery, graphic design basics, branding your business, and more.

For those who would like to know the design process and take control of their business' creative content, Canva is a great free resource for learning the basics and beyond. If designing all on your own still seems intimidating, here's where we will convince you that you can do it! The platform has tens of thousands of templates for a variety of marketing materials, including social media posts, invitations, posters, brochures, videos, infographics, flyers, business cards, and so much more.

While we have professional designers on our team, we are also huge proponents for Canva for our small business clients that want to take control of designing their assets.

We teach them how to make the most of this platform so they can succeed on their own. If you want our help building your brand in Canva, contact us at hello@francesroy to get started!

CHAPTER 1

Canva Tools and Functions with Illustrations

Canva offers a wide range of tools to help you create professional designs.

Please note: If you are using a smartphone, these tools and icons will be by the bottom of your phone screen on the canva interface.

Here's a list of Canva tools and a brief explanation of how to use them:

1. Text Tool: Use the text tool to add headings, paragraphs, and other text elements to your design.

How to locate: Simply click on the text tool icon by the left side of your canva design interface, a text editing window will display. Type your preferred text and select a font, size, and color.

Text

2. Shape Tool: The shape tool allows you to add various shapes, such as rectangles, circles, and triangles, to your design.

How to locate: Click on "Elements" by the left side tool bar of your canva interface, select the shape tool icon, select a preferred shape by clicking it, and it will appear on your design. These shapes are not editable so take time to choose one that best fits your design.

3. Image Tool: Use the image tool to upload your own images or search for free images from Canva's library.

How to locate: Click on "Uploads" on the tool bar by the left side of your canva interface, select image tool icon, select an image from your gallery, and click it to appear on your design.

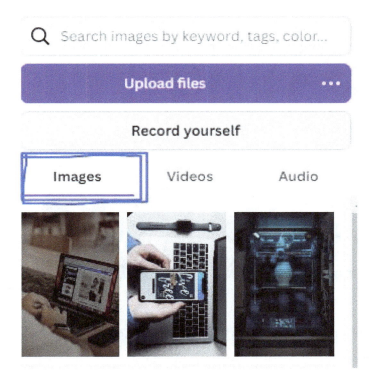

4. Graphic Tool: The graphic tool offers a range of pre-designed graphics, such as icons, logos, and illustrations. **How to locate:** Click on "Elements" by the left side toolbar of your canva interface, select the graphic tool icon, search and select a graphic, and click it to your design.

5. Video Tool: Use the video tool to add videos to your design. **How to locate:** Click on "Elements" by the left side toolbar of your canva interface, select the video tool icon, search and select a video using any preferred search term, and click it to your design.

6. Color Palette Tool: The color palette tool allows you to select a color scheme for your design.

How to locate: Click on text or element you want to change its color. A color palette window will appear at the top of the canva design page.

Click on your preferred color and apply it to your design until you are satisfied.

You can also use a color picker to choose any color an existing design.

Color

Q Try "blue" or "#00c4cc"

 Document colors

 Brand Kit

No brand colors set for this Brand Kit

 Default colors

Solid colors

7. Font Tool: Use the font tool to select a font for your text elements.

How to locate: Select the text you want to change its font. A text window will display at the top of the canva interface.

Click on the font tool icon, select your preferred font, and apply it to your text.

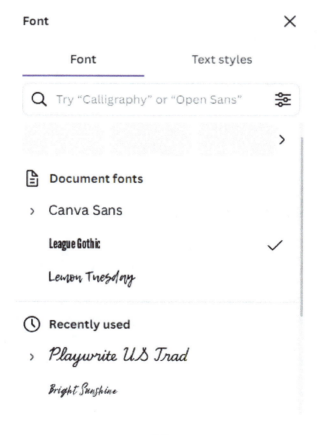

8. Resize Tool: The resize tool allows you to resize elements in your design or even your entire design. You can chage the size of your design from landscape to portrait or vice versa.

How to locate: Resize tool is located just on the top corner of your canva interface, immediately after the "File" icon.

Click on the resize tool icon, select an element, and input your preferred size.

Your design or element will change to the new size.

9. Rotate Tool: Use the rotate tool to rotate elements in your design.

How to locate: First click on the element, shape or text you want to rotate. The rotate tool will appear under or beside the element. Click on the rotate tool icon and drag it to your preferred angle to rotate.

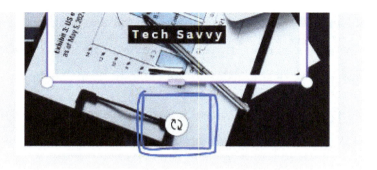

10. Flip Tool: The flip tool allows you to flip elements in your design. You can flip up, down, left or right.

How to locate: First select the element you want to flip on your design. A new toolbar will appear at the top right corner of your screen.

Click on the flip tool icon and select your preferred direction or angle to flip.

The element will flip on every click.

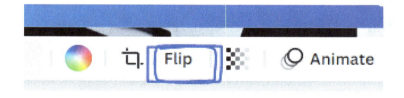

11. Duplicate Tool: Use the duplicate tool to duplicate elements in your design. If the need arises where you'll need two or more of the same element in your design, the duplicate tool can be of great help.

You can duplicate an element or an entire page. The process is relatively the same, with same icon.

How to locate: First click on the element you want to duplicate. It can be a text, picture, video or any other graphic piece. A new design window will appear right beside the element.

Locate the plus "+" sign and click it. The selected element will automatically be duplicated and you can use them sepearately on your designs.

You can also duplicate an entire page by clicking the plus "+" sign directly on the design canvas. The page will automatically be duplicated.

12. Alignment Tool: The alignment tool helps you align elements in your design. You can align text, images or other elements.

You can switch left, right, center or justify for texts.

How to locate: Click the text that you want to align. A toolbar will appear on the top of the page.

Click on the alignment tool icon and click to align. At every click, the text changes or adjusts to suit your selection.

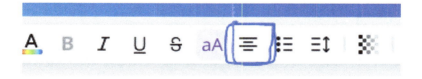

13. Layers Tool: Use the layers tool to manage the layers and elements in your design by placing them in front of or behind each other.

How to locate: First click the element that you want to switch its layer and a toolbar will appear at the top of the page.

Select position and click layers. You can now choose to arrange the elements behind or in front of eachother based on your preference by clicking until satisfied.

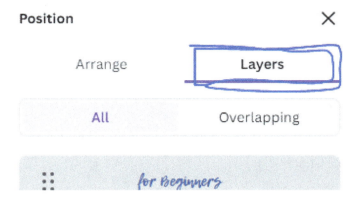

14. Group Tool: The group tool allows you to group different independent elements together to make them one, such that you can drag, move or edit more than one element at the same time.

How to locate: Select the fitst element and hold the "Shift key" on your keyboard. (If you are designing with a smartphone, click and hold the first element until you see a prompt that reads "Select Multiple").

Select the elements you want to group, and click to group. All the slected elements will be grouped as one.

15. Ungroup Tool: Use the ungroup tool to ungroup elements.

Just like the grouping, ungrouping elements is the direct opposite.

But you can't ungroup elements unless you have grouped them earlier.

So, to ungroups, just click the already grouped elements and a pop-up window will display.

Click ungroup and all the elements that was earlier grouped will be separated into their individual elements.

Click on the ungroup tool icon, select a group, and click to ungroup.

16. Background Tool: The background tool allows you to add a background image or color to your design. You can upload an image, and use it as the background of your design with just one click.

How to locate: You can just click on the design interface, select the color palette at the top of the page, and click a preferred backfround color. The background automatically changed to the selected color.

For image, you'll upload the image using the method explained in **"No. 3" above.** Right click on the uploaded image and select "Set image as background'. The image will automatically be set as your design background.

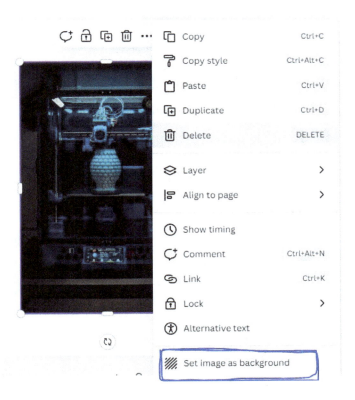

17. Grid Tool: Use the grid tool to create a grid system in your design.

A grid system helps you as the designer to place images or videos in a perfectly fitted form on the general design.

You can select a grid that matches your design and place your images neatly to get an appealing look.

How to locate: Click "Elements" on the left side of your canva design interface on your laptop.

On the search bar, type "grid".

Click on the grid tool icon, select "see all" to display all available grids, click on your preferred grid and it'll appear on your design interface, and apply images to fit.

← **Grids**

18. Ruler Tool: The ruler tool helps you measure and align elements in your design. This helps your design look accurate and appeling as all elements can have a unform size.

How to locate: Click on "File" on the top right corner of your canva design page. Hover your cursor to "setting" from the drop down and select "show rulers and guides".

You can also use the shortcut "Shift + R"

19. Undo Tool: Use the undo tool to undo changes in your design. As graphic designers, we must make mistakes while creating stunning designs.

This undo tool helps us back track our designs to the position it was before the mistake was made. The more you click the "undo" icon, it takes you to more previous designs.

How to locate: The undo icon is directly located on the blue toolbar at the top of the canva design interface.

Shortcut for Redo is "Ctrl + Z".

20. Redo Tool: The redo tool allows you to redo changes in your design. This is a perfect opposite of the "undo" icon.

As you click to take your design a step backward using the "undo" icon, you can click to also "redo" to take your designs a step forward.

How to locate: The redo icon is just beside the undo icon by the blue toolbar on the top of the canva design interface.

Shortcut for Redo is "Ctrl + Y".

By mastering these Canva tools, you'll be able to create professional designs with ease!

Getting Canva Right

Canva is a tool loaded with enough easy-to-use features and functionality that anyone can create a variety of engaging content that gets shared. These tools are helping small businesses get past two of the greatest obstacles to implementing an effective content marketing campaign: "Producing Engaging Content" and "Producing Content Consistently"

How Exactly Does Canva Work?

Canva allows you to sign-up and make an account completely free of cost. You have the option of logging in through your Gmail, Facebook, or email. Once you have logged in, you will be greeted by the Canva dashboard that features a search bar and a personal activities column on the left-hand side.

Once you click on the search bar, a dropdown menu will appear to guide you in whatever it is that you want to design. With Canva, you can also add multiple pages and layer them to create new effects for your posters. Once you are done with your design, you can simply download it in whatever format you want or schedule it for upload by connecting your social media outlet to the file.

You can also save the project file onto your dashboard and continue working on it later. Canva allows you to feel comfortable and choose the option that best fits your personal or company requirements.

Reasons Your Small Business Should Use Canva

Your small businesses needs high quality images. Canva can help. The world is a visual place. This has only become more true with new social media platforms and a shift to more engagement online. Your business must have high-quality branded images to compete, be seen, and succeed. If you've never designed before or are busy with other parts of your business, creating as many images as you need can feel overwhelming or like a low priority.

If this sounds like you, we recommend using Canva.

Canva is an online drag-and-drop image builder. Use Canva to design social media graphics, presentations, flyers, infographics, and much more.

Here are 8 reasons you should use Canva for your small business:

1. YOU CAN USE IT FOR FREE AND UPGRADING IS AFFORDABLE

Small businesses often have small marketing budgets - and every dollar counts in your bottom line.

Canva has an unlimited free account with many useful features. You get access to hundreds of templates, stock photos, icons, and other elements right away. In fact, for many small businesses, a free account is enough. But the free account does have limitations and restrictions.

Upgrading to the Pro account unlocks more templates, photos, elements, and fonts. You'll also gain features like saved brand colors, team members, and additional storage space.

The pro version starts at just $10 a month for the annual plan, which makes it much more affordable than many design programs or hiring an agency.

2. YOU DON'T NEED DESIGN EXPERIENCE - JUST AN EYE FOR WHAT YOU LIKE

Using Canva is the design equivalent of online shopping.

Whether you need a quote for social media, a flyer for a sale, or a full presentation for your pitch, Canva has ready-to-use templates. Just search for the project you're working on and browse for a template you like. It's easy to change the colors and fonts to match your brand. You can also add your logo and photos to brand it further.

You can even use Canva to build your own custom designs. If you have design experience or want more control, start with a blank page and add your own elements, typography, and more. Canva is a drag-and-drop editor that's intuitive to use and quick to learn.

If you're comfortable using the internet and programs like Mircosoft Word or PowerPoint, you'll enjoy using Canva. They also have a large online library of articles that teach you how to use tools and features. And as a bonus, their blog is a great resource for other design topics like finding font pairings, choosing colors, and more.

3. ACCESS YOUR PROJECTS FROM ANYWHERE AND ON YOUR PHONE

Because Canva is an online service, it stores your designs in the cloud. That means you can start a project at home and continue working on it in your shop or office. It's much easier to design on a laptop or computer than a phone.

But the Canva app makes it quick to upload and use photos you took with your phone. You can also save your images and share directly to your social media pages from the app.

4. THEY HAVE STOCK PHOTOS, ICONS, FONTS, ELEMENTS, AND MORE READY TO USE

You're busy. Spend less time hunting for the perfect photo and assets for your project. Canva has thousands of photos and elements available immediately after you start. The best thing is Canva manages the licenses for the photos and assets. That means you can create something and feel confident that you can use it for your business. If you want even more elements, upgrade to the Pro account.

5. SEND LINKS AND WORK WITH OTHERS

Share your designs with others by creating a link to your project. Invite people to a comment-only mode or give them full permission to edit the design. Easily get feedback or help from coworkers and trusted friends. If you have someone take over design for your business, they can also use share links to send you designs for review and approval.

6. YOU DON'T HAVE TO KEEP UP WITH RECOMMENDED SOCIAL MEDIA SIZES

Social media platforms are always changing the ideal ratios for posts and graphics. If you're tired of looking up what each platform wants every time you create an image, let

Canva do the work for you. All you'll need to do is choose the platform and Canva will set up a page that's the current recommended size. You'll finish before you would have even started without the program.

7. AUTOMATICALLY RESIZE YOUR DESIGNS

You've created a beautiful Facebook image but now you need to create a Pinterest pin and an image for your website banner, and another for your blog. With the pro account, the resize tool automatically converts your design to other sizes. This is so useful and saves so much time. If you have the free account, you can always create different sized documents and copy design elements manually.

8. CREATE BRAND CONSISTENCY AND SAVE TIME

One of the best features of Canva is how easy it is to duplicate and edit your graphics. That means you can easily replicate graphics with new content. Cultivating a consistent look through template choice, color, and font helps you build better brand awareness and stand out. Canva helps you stay consistent because you can copy pages and designs. Canva can also be used to batch process items.

This is when you create many graphics to drip out over time. For example, if you know you want to share a quote graphic every Monday, you don't have to create a quote design every Monday. Instead, build a Canva template. Then duplicate the page and update the quote as many times as you want. Save all these images. Now you have content ready to be used for weeks to come.

Pro tip: Did you know you can have more than one template in each document? If you find more than one template for your project, drag them onto separate pages. Now you have more variety among your images and one easy to manage file. If you're a small business starting or upgrading your marketing and design, Canva is a useful solution and tool. It's affordable. It's easy. It's powerful. And since you can start for free, isn't it worth trying?

Difference Between Free and Pro

If you don't use Canva often then the free version is more than sufficient and has some great tools. However if you use it frequently, really want to create consistency and get a bit more creative with it then the $14.99 per month is well worth the investment.

The benefits of having the pro version are;

• **You get a 'Brand Kit',** where you can upload your logo in all formats, your specific brand colours and codes and the fonts you use. Therefore when you create any document in Canva it will automatically pull those options through first and to the top, one saving you time and two creating complete consistency across all your literature and marketing.

• **Unlimited Folders** – with the free version you get two folders where you can file and organise the documents you have created, on the paid version you get unlimited folders. As an example I have different folders for different clients I create documents for, I have one for my social media templates, one for client proposals and so on. It makes it easier to find your designs and makes it much more organised.

• **Background Remover** – if you have a photo or image you want to use but don't want to use the background, in the old days it would be spending hours in Paint manually removing the image, but with Canva Pro you can literally click a button and it removes the background for you.

• **Re-sizing** – If you want to have the correct size images for the specific platform without having to duplicate and recreate the designs, there is a resize button which allows you to select an existing design and at the click of a button re-size that image for another chosen platform, like an Insta post can be resized to Facebook.

• **Access to a huge library of fonts and images** - On the free version you have access to a number of fonts and images, however many are restricted and you have to pay extra for if you want to use them. The pro version you have access to hundreds more options, meaning you can personalise your designs more and save time searching for images on sites such as Pixabay and Pexels. So you see, Canva is such a fantastic tool that doesn't have to cost you a penny, however it is well work the £10.99 per month for the pro version (which if you do monthly you can cancel at any time). It will make marketing your business easier, save you time and create brand consistency.

PRICING

Canva offers its users three different pricing plans with distinct features for each one.

Each plan offers a free trial, so you can make an informed decision before the purchase. Additionally, Canva offers its premium versions for free to registered nonprofits and schools. The details for each of the individual user plans are listed below:

1. Free Plan

• Billed at 0$ monthly and annually

• 8000+ free templates

• 100+ design types (social media posts, presentations, and others)

• Hundreds of thousands of free photos and graphics

• Create designs with custom dimensions

• Full collaboration access including team sharing, edit access and built-in commenting

• 1 GB cloud storage with 2 folders

• Two-factor authentication

2. Pro Plan

• Billed at $12.95 per month and $9.95 per user per month for a yearly subscription

• All free plan features

• Customized logos, colors, and fonts in 1 brand kit

- One-click design resize

- 60,000+ free templates

- 60+ million premium stock images, videos, and graphics

- Upload your own fonts and logos

- Custom templates

- Customizable download quality

- 100 GB cloud storage with unlimited folders

- 24/7 support availability

3. Enterprise Plan

- Billed at $30 per user per month for a yearly subscription

- For other billing options, contact the sales team

- All pro plan features

- Customized logos, colors, and fonts across multiple brand kits

- Control what team members can see, upload and access with brand controls

- Built-in workflows to get approval on designs

- Protect any part of your design from team edits

- Advanced template locking

- Unlimited storage

- Unlimited folders

- Single-sign on (SSO)

- 24/7 Enterprise level control

Pros and Cons of Canva

Pros

• Canva offers a very interactive and user-friendly interface that is easy to navigate.

• It offers pre-made templates, even in the free version.

• The software offers a free trial period for each of its plans to make an informed decision when paying for the subscription.

• It makes it easier for social marketers to strategize media schedules

• Designing flyers, brochures, posters, and other marketing content becomes readily available.

• It can create an entire series of Instagram stories, save it, and even upload it at a scheduled time.

• Canva is a multi-purpose platform that can help create marketing content and photo editing and custom template designing that can be used for whatever you want.

• This platform is also great for teams as it allows collaborative functionality and can easily manage workflow operations.

• There are a host of available options for digital editing, design, and collaborations that can optimize the quality of your work.

• Canva has 24/7 available support, which makes it easier for users to remain productive at all times.

Cons

• Pre-set image sizes are sometimes too large or out of frame when posting content

• The mobile app does not hold the same functionality as the desktop version.

• The free plan does not come with 24/7 support.

• The free version does not assure quality templates.

How much money can canva save small businesses?

As a startup business, expect to spend anywhere from $500 to $2000 on graphic design expenses during your company's formation.

Digital designs don't end there. After all, you want to keep your growing social media audience entertained and engaged, right? That means plenty of simple graphics.

CHAPTER 2

Most Important Canva Design Tools Explained

Let us take a closer look on the most important tools for all graphic designers. The faster you get familiar with these tools, the better because you'll start creating stunning designs fast.

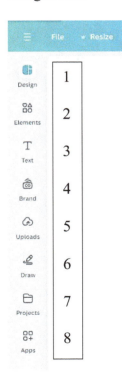

As a beginner, understanding Canva tools can seem overwhelming, but mastering them can bring numerous benefits to your design journey.

Here are some of the tools, how to use them, and their benefits.

Getting Started with Basic Canva Toolbar for Beginners and Businesses

1. Design Icon:

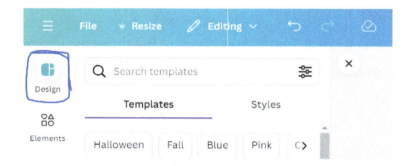

This icon carries a large directory of design templates that designers can choose from and edit to suit their own preference. It is easy to locate by the top left corner of the canva screen for PC and at the bottom of the screen for smartphone users.

Once you open a new design layout to start creating a design, you can click on the Design icon to see a range of other similar design templates. The most interesting of it is that you can even search using the search bar, based on your design term, to get beautiful editable templates. Just click the one you like, and edit the information on it to suit your own design.

2. Elements Icon:

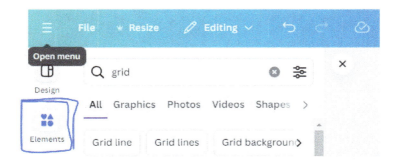

This is one of the most important icon on the canva interface as it has a bunch of functions with special features.

Inside this "Elements icon" you'll find a search bar, where you can input any search term you want to use in your design.

For example: If you are working on a party flyer that requires picture of a lady holding a cup of wine, just click on Elements by the left side of your canva design screen, and search "pretty white lady holding a cup of wine".

This will load and display hundreds of pretty white ladies holding a cup of wine.

You can choose the one that fits your design, click it to appear on your design, and use it as you want on the design.

3. Text Tool

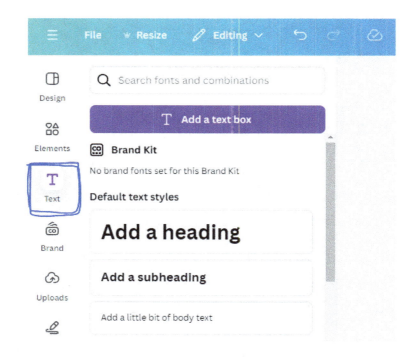

The text tool is responsible for writing all forms or types of words on your design. Just click on the "T" icon by the left side of canva interface, the text toolbox will display.

Select your preferred text template by clicking it, and it'll appear on your design. Edit the text to suit what you want to write on the design and place it where you want. You can also change fonts, size or rotate to fit your perferece too.

4. Brand Icon

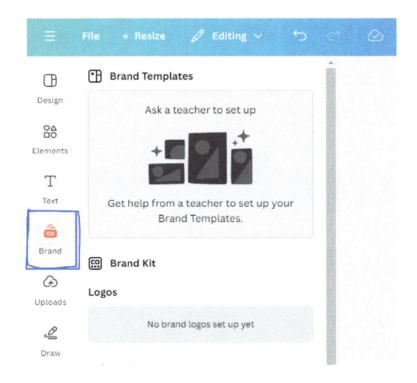

This is a special canva feature that helps automate your design process. The Brand icon lets you set customizable presets for easy access of constantly used elements when designing.

You can add brand logos, fonts, voice, etc. so anytime you have to use these elements, instead of going into your gallery to look for these elements everytime, you can just set it under this brand as a preset and click to use anytime you want.

To configure this, just click on the Brand icon by the left corner of your canva interface, and start customization by clicking on each icon and uploading each element.

5. Uploads Icon

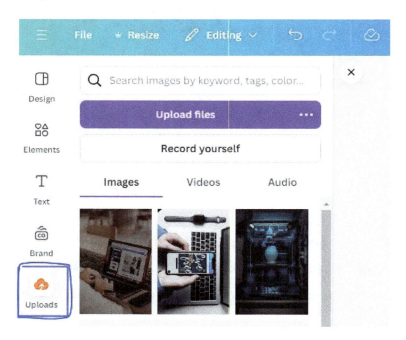

Here's one of the most underrated canva icon.

This "Uploads" icon is responsible for helping you add third party images and videos to your designs.

If you have a special picture or video to add to your design, it is the uploads icon that will be used import the picture or video into canva, before it is placed on your design.

To use this feature, click the "Uploads icon" by the left side of your canva interface and select whether you want to upload picture, video or audio.

Select the correct icon and it will take you to your system gallery to choose the file you want to import into canva.

Click on your preferred media file and it will be uploaded into the canva interface. Now you can click the file to appear on your design and use it to fit.

You can also copy your media file from your gallery by right clicking on the media file, and selecting "copy".

After copying the file (picture, video or audio), you can now open your canva app, locate your design, right click on it, and click paste. The media file will automatically be imported into your design. This is a shortcut form of copying or importing file into your designs.

Shortcut for copying is "Ctrl + C" while to paste is "Ctrl + V".

6. Draw Icon

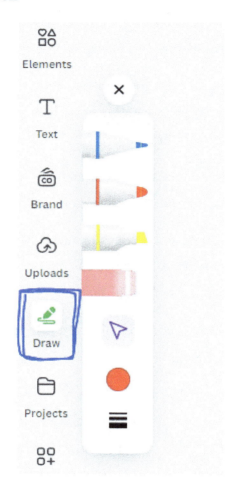

This feature allows you to draw patterns on your designs. You can select from any of the pen tools, and use it to draw any type of pattern you want on your design.

Locate and click the "Draw" icon by the side of your canva interface, and another toolbar will display.

Select your preferred drawing pen, and use it to create any type of pattern you want on your design.

7. Project Icon

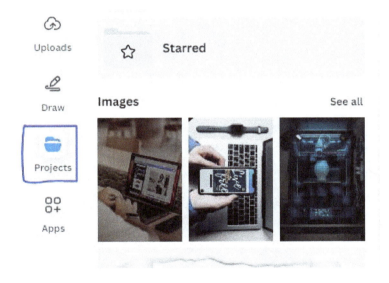

Here you can access all your previous projects by arranging them in a single project file and saving under the project icon section of your canva interface.

Just click the project icon by the left side of your canva interface, select project and start saving all you customizable elemnts for easy access on your next project.

8. Apps Icon

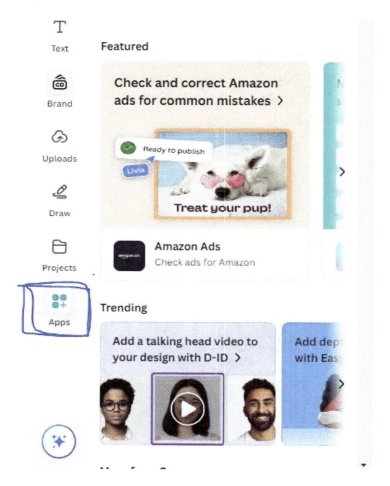

The Apps icon gives you access to third party applications that are partnering with canva to make your design journey smooth. You need to get familiar with some app functions for you to know how to use them.

Some of these apps include, mockups, cartoonify, language translators, voice changers, etc.

You can access these apps by clicking on the "Apps" icon by the left side of your canva screen.

Search the app you want or choose from a wide range of apps in the "Discover" section.

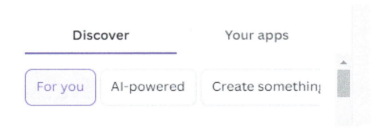

Click on your preferred app and follow the prompt to learn how to use it.

The process is really self explanatory.

Getting Started with Canva Designing

When you start a small business, it's common for you to take on many roles in your business including graphic design since there is this fantastic free tool called Canva where you can easily create beautiful graphics.

Canva will allow you to create professional graphics for social media, your blog, your website, proposals, powerpoint etc.

You can use a large part of Canva for free or subscribe to the pro account for even more capabilities at just a low $12.95 per month.

It is an absolute game changer for small business, which is why I am so excited to share this blog with you. Right let's get started!

Before you jump into creating your design, take some time to think about what you are creating and who you are creating it for.

1. Purpose

What are you making? Is it an infographic or poster? Or a social media post? Is it an assignment or for a personal project?

If it is for an assignment, take a moment to read over the assignment instructions and then think about the purpose of your visual document.

What message are you creating and what will you use to communicate it?

2. Audience

It may be that you are working on an assignment for a course, but the answer is probably more than just your professor.

Think about why your instructor is asking you to create your project and who the audience could be.

What does this audience already know?

What is the audience interested in?

Do they have a specific vocabulary you should draw from? Or are you trying to be as open as possible in your language?

Think about what your audience wants and make sure your design meets that need.

3. Plan

Design is about using colour, graphics and text to communicate a message.

Brainstorm ideas about the text, graphics and layout you want to include.

Think about colour combinations and fonts.

Remember that this is just a plan and it can change as you begin to create it.

4. Explore

Once you have a basic plan and outline, you can explore Canva, or a different tool, to see how you can make your plan become a reality.

Take time to see what graphics are available in the free version and determine if you will need to find different images or graphics outside the library in Canva.

Use the Find Audio, Images and Videos for remixing guide to know where to search.

5. Create

Start creating your design in Canva

Pro Tip: make sure you select the proper dimensions from the beginning.

You can't resize a project in the free version of Canva.

6. Share

Canva allows you to export in PDF, PNG, and JPEG without a watermark.

How to Set Up a Free Canva Account

You can create a new Canva account at www.canva.com for free.

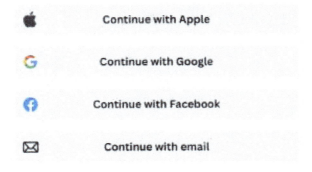

There are four different options for signing up:

• Facebook

• Apple

• Google

• Email

Select your preferred method and continue by following the signup prompt.

Update the following:

• Profile Name (Add your Business Name and Purpose here)

• Handle — this will ultimately be your URL for example http://canva.com/8020lwtte

• Website URL

• State

• Country

How do I start a new project?

To edit a readymade Canva design:

1. After logging in to Canva, select 'Create a design' in the top right-hand corner.

2. Browse the design categories to choose the one you'd like to create (poster, presentation, logo, etc.).

3. A new tab will appear with the blank design you've chosen.

4. Start designing by browsing and selecting one of Canva's ready made layouts (optional and customizable), or start with a blank design and add in your own original background, images and text.

To create a Canva design with custom dimensions

1. Click 'Create a design', select 'custom dimensions' at the bottom of the menu.

2. Input the width and height you'd like your design to be in pixels (px), millimeters (mm) or inches (in)

3. A new tab will appear with your blank design.

When creating a custom design, you will not have access to Canva's readymade layout templates.

How is the design page organized?

The design page is divided into two main sections.

The right side of your page is your workspace. Here, you will see the page you are working on.

You can use the slider in the bottom right-hand corner of your page to zoom in and out of your design.

The left side of your screen is your toolbar.

You can click through the navigation bar to access:

• Templates

• Elements

• Uploads

• Text

Click "More" at the bottom of your navigation bar to explore the other available tools you can use for your design, including:

- Photos

- Styles

- Audio

- Videos

- Background

- Charts

- Folders

By selecting any of these options, you can add them to your main navigation menu on the left.

How to change the design background

1. Select 'Background' from the left navigation menu (or from 'More').

2. For a solid colour background, select a colour at the top of the background menu.

You can also create a custom colour here by clicking on the colour palette icon next to the solid colour choices.

You can also select or create a solid colour by clicking on your design then clicking the colour square above it.

3. If you want a design for your background, select from the free options provided by Canva (located below the colour options).

How to add images, shapes, lines, etc

1. Select 'Elements' from the left navigation menu.

2. Choose one of the options that appears i.e. shapes, lines, grids, etc.

If you are looking for a specific image, you can also type the keyword into the search bar and Canva will gather a bunch of results to choose from.

3. Click or drag the element to have it appear in your design.

4. Select the element within your design and drag the corners inward and outward to change the size. You will know when you have selected your element because a blue box will appear around it.

5. Within your design, you can change the size, location, colour and orientation of the element you added using the menu that appears above your page.

Note: There are both free and premium (paid for) elements. Elements will be clearly marked as free or with a price ($).

If you include premium features in your design, it will prompt you to pay when you download your design.

To delete elements on your design

1. Select the element you want to delete.

2. Hit the 'backspace' or 'delete' key on your keyboard, or select the trash icon in the top menu of the design window.

How to add your own images

1. Select 'Uploads' from the left navigation menu.

2. Click 'Upload media'.

3. Select the files you would like to upload from your computer, then click open.

4. Once the image has fully uploaded, click it to add it to your design.

How to set an image as design background

1. Right-click on the image you want to use as your background.

2. At the bottom of the pop-up menu, select 'Set image as background'.

How do I adjust the transparency of an image or element?

To adjust the transparency of an item in your design:

1. Click on the item you want to adjust until it is highlighted in blue.

2. In the toolbar across the top of the screen, click on 'Transparency'.

3. Use the slider tool to adjust the transparency of your item.

How to change the order of my images

You can adjust the way your items and images layer with one another by changing the order of your items.

• Right click on the image you want to move. A menu will appear with layering options for the image.

'Send to back' will put your image at the back of your design, with all other items appearing on top of it.

'Send Backward' will send your image back by one layer.

'Bring Forward' will bring your image forward by one layer

'Bring to front' will place your image at the very front of your design, in front of all other images.

• Adjusting the order of your images will help your design make visual sense.

How to group or ungroup images

To group images so that they remain stuck together:

1. Highlight the elements you want to be grouped together. Once highlighted, an option to 'group' will appear in the toolbar at the top of the screen.

2. Select 'group' to stick your images together into one.

To ungroup these elements:

1. Click on the group until it is highlighted in blue.

2. Click 'Ungroup' in the toolbar at the top of the screen.

Your images will now be independent from one another again.

In a template, it is common that a lot of elements will be grouped automatically.

If you want to change the layout of your design by ungrouping these elements, right-click on the section you want to ungroup, and select 'ungroup' in the pop-up menu.

Your elements should now be independent from each other. To re-group your elements in a template, highlight the elements you want to be grouped together until they are highlighted in blue.

Then, right-click. In the pop-up menu, select 'group.'

How to add text

1. Select 'text' from the left navigation menu.

2. Click or drag heading, subheading or body text to add it to your design.

3. Change the size, colour, font, orientation and organization of your text using the top menu above your design.

How to change text from lowercase to uppercase?

1. Begin by adding a heading, subheading, or textbox to your design.

2. In the tool bar across the top of the screen, click on the ellipses (...) to view more advanced text options.

3. Click on the uppercase tool to convert your text from lowercase to uppercase, or from uppercase to lowercase.

How to use HTML colour code

HTML colour codes are a unique combination of numbers and letters that code for a specific colour.

This step is useful when creating designs for particular brands, as most major brands have specific colours that they use to make sure everything they create and post appears cohesive.

For example, the University of Guelph has a colour palette that represents the University brand, and each of these colours have a different code. For this example, we will use Guelph Red.

1. Begin by clicking on the colour square above your design to open up the colour options.

2. In the search bar at the top, insert the colour code you are looking for.

3. The particular colour you need should appear.

4. You can also use HTML colour codes to change the colour of text or particular elements.

To explore Canva's ready-made colour palettes

1. Select 'Styles' from the left navigation menu (or from 'More').

2. Select 'Colors'

3. Click on a colour palette to use it in your design.

How to add another page to Canva design?

1. Select the 'Add a new page' button underneath the last page in your design.

2. A new page will appear underneath the current page.

To add a new page and duplicate the design of the previous page:

1. Select the 'duplicate page' icon, located at the top of each page in the design.

2. A new page with the same design will appear underneath the current page.

To delete pages

1. Scroll to the page you want to delete.

2. Select the trash icon located at the top of each page of the design

How to rename design?

1. Put your cursor in the box that reads 'Add a heading' at the top of the Canva window.

2. Type a new name for your design.

3. Hit 'Enter' on your keyboard.

How to collaborate with others on a design

To share my design via an email invite

1. Select 'Share' from the top of the Canva window.

2. Enter the email addresses of those you'd like to collaborate with on your design.

3. Select the permissions you'd like the collaborators to have: either 'can edit' or 'can view.'

4. Click 'send invites' to complete.

To share my design via a link

1. Select 'Share' from the top right hand corner of the Canva window.

2. Select the permissions you'd like the collaborators to have: either 'to edit' or 'to view.'

3. Copy the link directly in the share box and send it to your collaborators.

Collaborators can use the notes and comment feature to provide feedback for each page of your design.

How to download your final design

1. Select the 'Download' icon from the top menu in the Canva window.

2. From the dropdown menu that appears, select the file type (JPEG, PNG, PDF Standard, or PDF for printing). Also select whether you want to download all pages of the design, or just select pages.

3. Click 'Download.' The file should appear in the 'downloads' folder on your computer.

Embed your design using HTML

1. Make your design public: turn on the 'Public' feature from the top menu in the Canva window.

2. Select 'Share' from the top menu.

3. Select 'Embed' from the new window that appears.

4. Copy the HTML code from the window and place it where you want to embed your design.

CHAPTER 3

Creating a Design From Scratch on Canva

On the Canva homepage, click the '**Create a design**' button.

You will then see a variety of template sizes, and types or you can choose to create your own custom design.

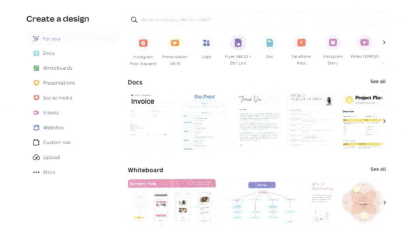

For this example, let us use Instagram Post which is 1080 x 1080 px. You will then have a blank canvas to design whatever you like.

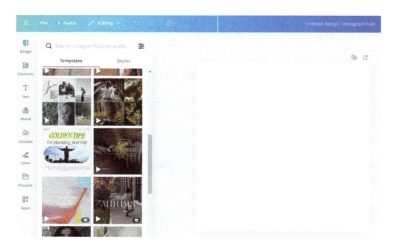

1. Uploading an image

To upload your own images into Canva, click 'Uploads' and then click the 'Upload media' button.

You will see the option to upload from your device, Dropbox, Google drive, Instagram and Facebook, and upload your image from there.

2. Using effects on images and removing background

Once you have chosen an image to add to your design,

Select your image within the design and click on >effects >background remover (BG Remover). This will automatically remove the background and keep the main part of your image.

This effect is impressively accurate but if necessary, you can also use the 'Erase' and 'Restore' buttons to fix up any areas of the image.

By removing the background on images, you can get creative with your image edits and add either a new background or a simple backdrop colour like below as an example.

To do this click on the white part of the canvas where you have removed the background > then go to background colour > from there select the colour you want from the left hand panel shown below.

3. Adding text on your design

Click 'Text', and add either a heading, subheading or body text. Simply drag the desired type of text across onto your design. Once you have added a text, you can make additional adjustments by either changing the font, colour, size, effects and more.

You can also add dot points for your text too, which is perfect if you're creating a flyer or a document.

4. Adding a logo

To add your logo into Canva, you can upload it the same way as uploading an image. Go to uploads > images > located your logo and drag it across onto your graphic you are designing.

If your logo has a white background, you can also use the background remover here to give it a more professional look on your design.

5. Brand Kits

As you may know, the way your brand looks and feels is extremely important when communicating your product, service or message.

Canva can help you keep your brand identity consistent just by setting up a simple brand kit.

Here you can set up an easy reference for your brand by having your logo, fonts, colours and images all set up and ready to refer to when creating any new designs or content for your brand.

6. Setting up your brand kit

To start setting up your brand kit, click on the 'brand kit' button on the left of your home screen.

7. Brand Logo

The first thing you can do to set up your brand kit is add in your logo. Your logo is likely to be used in nearly every design you create so it's a great time saver to have a transparent logo ready to go in your brand kit.

Simply click the plus button to upload your saved logo.

8. Brand colours

Next, choose the colours that make up your brand identity and have that exact shade ready to go with every design.

Again, just press the plus button and choose the exact shades that make up your brand identity so you're always staying consistent with your colour palette.

9. Brand Fonts

Setting up your brand kit will help give you more clarity and make future edits simple and easy when using Canva.

Using existing templates

No matter what it is you're wanting to create, Canva's templates are completely customisable, easy to use, and give you a great amount of inspiration.

Firstly, you will see a large variety of templates to choose from on the homepage of your Canva account.

Otherwise, you can click on 'Templates' and use the search bar to find a template category for what you're trying to create. There's a great amount of options to choose from.

For the purpose of this blog, I have chosen a random template for an instagram story that I can completely customise with the help of my brand kit.

As previously shown, you can upload your own picture and replace the template picture given.

If you don't have any pictures to upload, you can also click on 'photos' and search for any of the pictures that Canva offers for you to add onto your design.

Drag and drop your desired photo onto your template like I have done in the image below.

Next, you can click on any part of the design and change the colours with the help of your brand kit.

Click on the background of your design and the little coloured square on the top left corner to change the colours. You will see your brand kit colours appear.

To add a title and a subtitle, click text and add a text to your page. When you want to change the fonts, the uploaded fonts in your brand kit will appear and be ready to use or you can pick a font on Canva as mentioned earlier.

10. Finding creative elements to use

Canva also has thousands of elements to choose from and add to your designs.

You can search through these by going to Elements, then by typing in relevant words to suit the type of element you're after.

It might also be worth researching Canva elements that are on trend too.

Some great elements or texts at the moment include; Newbrushstroke, Bloggerdoodle, Freeformpro, and block lady.

You may also be able to see that editing on canva will even allow you to add audio or video to your designs. Depending on your business and designs, this could be a great way to edit designs and stand out from the crowd.

11. Saving your templates

Don't forget to save your amazing designs so that you can use them again and stay consistent with your brand. Canva will autosave as you go. And then once you've finished a design, go to the homepage and click 'your designs.

Click the three dots on the top right of your image and then click 'move to folder'. This function allows you to save the design in a folder so that you can refer straight back to it and easily copy it for another similar design you want to create.

Must-Know Canva Hacks for Small Business Owners

Even though we have backgrounds in design and using fancier software, Canva has taken care of the majority of our graphic design needs for the past 7+ years. From experience over the years we've been using Canva, there are at least 10 must-know hacks every creative small business owner needs to know!

1. Move Elements Freely

By default, Canva will snap elements in certain positions based on its alignment with other elements or the background.

While this is super helpful in most cases, sometimes it's just downright annoying when you want to place an element in a position, but Canva keeps snapping it somewhere else.

To solve this, when you click and hold your element to move it, press and hold the Command key on Mac (Cntrl for Windows) to be able to move your element around freely.

2. Find Photos with Your Brand Colors

Instead of searching for images with keywords like "blue desk" or "pink flowers" to hopefully find something that's similar enough to your brand colors to use, just use your hex codes! In the Photos tab search bar, click the sliders icon > the + sign under "Color" > copy and paste one of your brand color's hex code to find photos with that color in them.

There are even other filters you can add, like the photo orientation, price, and a toggle for cut-out images (images with a transparent background).

3. Find Similar Elements that You Like

Have you ever found an element you really liked in a design but have trouble finding others that are similar to it? When you add an element to your design, select it and then click the "i" button to show information about the element.

Then, you can either click the artist's name to view their other works or choose "See more like this" to see similar elements!

4. View Images from the Same Photographer

Similar to #3, it's super easy to find photos from the same photographer that you may like. If you find a photo you like in the search menu, hover over the image to click the three dots, then click "View more by [Artist Name]" to view their other works!

5. Remove Photo Backgrounds

Removing backgrounds from photos to use in designs can really make images pop in your graphics.

To do so, add a photo to your design > click Edit in the top menu bar > find Background Remover.

From there, you can erase or restore with a brush (and size adjustment) to get it as close to perfect as you want (although we have to say Canva does a pretty great job from the jump.)

6. Add Shadows or Outlines to Photos

To really make an image pop in your designs, Canva allows you to easily add shadows or outlines to your 2D photos. In the same way you click Edit to find the Background Remover, there's also Shadows with a selection of various shadow positions and options.

If you hover over an option and click the slider icon, you can even make further adjustments to the shadow, like offset, transparency, blur, and color.

7. Easily Create Design Mockups

Canva does it once again with the smart design options for photos! This time, instead of Background Remover or Shadows, we're going to look for either Smart Mockups or Frames.

Frames has a selection of solely devices and different style frames, whereas Smart Mockups includes things like devices on desks, phones in hands, mugs, t-shirts, cards, etc. Even if the mockup you choose has an angle, Canva will automatically adjust the photo to fit and look as natural as possible.

8. Import & Edit PDFs

Possibly one of our fav Canva hacks is that you can import PDFs to edit, too! You aren't limited to only uploading photos or elements to use in designs. On the Canva homepage, once you click to create a new design, select Import File instead to choose a PDF. You'll be able to edit text and font styles, drag and rearrange elements, change colors, and more!

9. Share or Collaborate with a Team or Client

If you have a team or you like to give clients access to design files as you're working on them, Canva makes sharing and collaborating especially easy!

When you hover over a design on the Canva homepage and click the three dots, you can Share your design with others (or you can click the Share button in the top-right corner inside the design file). You can add specific people by email or create a link to send elsewhere. If you create a public link, you can choose whether people who access the file can edit, view only, or comment only.

Those you share it with (if they have the permission) can add comments on either the page as a whole or on specific elements within the design. You can even @mention someone else on the team or who has access to the file.

10. Organize Designs in Folders

Not only can you organize your uploads into folders, like images, you can organize whole designs.

When you're creating a new design in Canva, you're able to choose past designs to import.

So if you start a new file and realize you want to mirror a design you've created in the past, you'll be able to easily import specific pages from that design into the one you're working on now.

That's just one instance of the many possibilities of organization when it comes to folders in Canva!

How to Use Canva as a Business Owner

As a business owner, having visually appealing graphics and designs is crucial for creating brand recognition, engaging with customers, and promoting your products or services. Hiring a professional graphic designer or using expensive design software may not always be feasible though, especially for small businesses or startups. That's where Canva comes in.

This popular and user-friendly online graphic design tool allows business owners to create professional-looking designs without extensive design skills or a big budget.

If you have a tablet and a touchscreen pen, or just a regular computer, you have all you need to get started. In this blog, we'll explore how to use Canva as a business owner, including tips and tricks on creating stunning graphics for all sorts of purposes.

Familiarize Yourself with Canva's Features

Canva offers a wide range of features and tools that can help you create a variety of designs for social media posts, business cards, presentations, and more.

Take some time to familiarize yourself with its interface, icons, and design elements. Explore the different design types, templates, fonts, colors, and images available in the extensive library. Canva also offers premium elements and features for a fee, so be mindful of what is free and what requires a subscription or payment.

Choose the Right Template

Canva offers thousands of pre-designed templates for various design purposes, such as social media posts, presentations, posters, flyers, and more. These templates are a great starting point for creating professional-looking designs quickly and easily. Begin by selecting a template that matches your design needs and style preferences.

You can then customize it by changing the text, images, colors, and fonts to align with your brand identity.

Customize With Your Branding

As a business owner, it's essential to maintain consistent branding across all your marketing materials. Canva allows you to upload your brand logo, colors, and fonts, which you can then use in your designs.

Customizing your graphics with your branding elements creates a cohesive look and feel for your business, ensuring that they are aligned with your brand identity. Consistent branding helps establish brand recognition and builds trust with your audience.

Add Engaging Visuals

Visuals play a crucial role in creating eye-catching and engaging designs.

Canva offers a vast library of images, icons, illustrations, and other visual elements that you can use to enhance your graphics. You can search for specific images or use filters to find images that match your design concept.

Be mindful of using high-quality visuals that are relevant to your business and resonate with your target audience.

You can also upload your own images or use Canva's background remover tool to remove backgrounds from images and create custom visuals.

Customize Text and Fonts

Text is an essential element in many designs, whether it's for social media posts, infographics, or presentations.

Canva provides a wide range of font options that you can use to customize your text and make it visually appealing.

Experiment with different fonts, sizes, and styles to create text that is easy to read and complements your branding.

You can also adjust the spacing, alignment, and color of your text to create a visually pleasing layout.

Utilize the Collaborative Features

If you have a team or multiple stakeholders involved in your design process, Canva's collaborative features can be very useful.

Canva allows you to invite team members to work together on a design in real-time, making it easy to get feedback, make edits, and finalize the design together.

You can also share completed designs with clients' or team members for review or approval.

Canva's collaborative features streamline the design process to ensure that everyone involved is on the same page.

Save and Share Your Designs

Once you have created your design, Canva allows you to save and download it in various file formats, such as JPEG, PNG, PDF, or GIF.

You can also share your designs directly from Canva to social media platforms, email, or other communication channels.

This makes it easy to export and share your designs in the format that suits your needs, whether they're intended for online or offline use.

Canva is a powerful tool that can be a game-changer for business owners who want to create professional-looking graphics without the need for extensive design skills or a big budget.

With its user-friendly interface, collaborative features, and extensive library of templates, images, and fonts, it provides a creative and efficient way to design graphics that align with your brand identity and engage with your target audience.

By following the tips and best practices outlined in this blog, you can utilize Canva effectively to elevate your visual marketing game.

So, go ahead and explore Canva's features to customize your brand designs and share them conveniently and confidently.

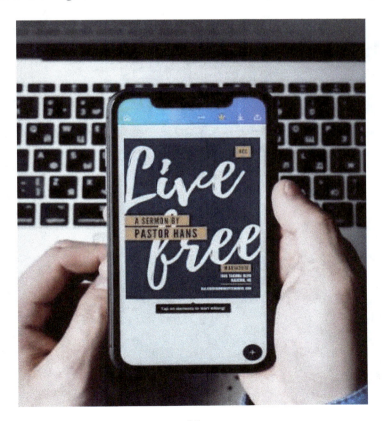

CHAPTER FOUR

Designing a Business Card on Canva: A Step-by-Step Guide

Sign in: Log in to your Canva account or create a new one.

Search: Type "business card" in the search bar and select the "Business Card" template.

Choose a template: Browse through Canva's vast template library and select a design that suits your style.

Customize: Tailor the template to your liking by changing the layout, colors, fonts, and elements.

Add your details: Insert your name, title, company, contact information, and social media handles.

Upload your logo: Add your company logo or create a new one using Canva's logo maker.

Edit text: Modify the font styles, sizes, and colors to match your brand.

Add images: Incorporate relevant images or graphics to enhance the design.

Adjust layout: Rearrange elements to achieve a balanced and visually appealing design.

Download: Save your design as a PDF, JPG, or PNG file.

Print: Send your design to a printer or order prints directly from Canva.

Tips and Variations:

Use a consistent color scheme and font style to maintain your brand identity.

Experiment with different shapes, such as rounded corners or a circular design.

Add a QR code or NFC chip for digital connectivity.

Incorporate a tagline or mission statement to convey your company's values.

Create a double-sided design for extra space or visual impact.

Use Canva's "Resize" feature to adapt your design for different formats, like a mini business card or a networking card.

Best Practices:

Keep your design clean and simple to ensure readability.

Use a standard font size (around 10-12 points) for easy scanning.

Leave sufficient white space to avoid clutter.

Ensure your logo is legible and centered.

Double-check for spelling and grammar errors.

Designing a Logo with Canva: A Step-by-Step Guide

Sign in: Log in to your Canva account or create a new one.

Search: Type "logo" in the search bar and select the "Logo" template.

Choose a template: Browse through Canva's vast template library and select a design that inspires you.

Customize: Tailor the template to your liking by changing the layout, colors, fonts, and elements.

Add text: Insert your company name or a meaningful phrase.

Add a symbol: Choose an icon or graphic that represents your brand.

Experiment with fonts: Select a font that resonates with your brand's personality.

Color palette: Pick a color scheme that reflects your brand's values and emotions.

Edit and refine: Adjust the design elements until you're satisfied.

Download: Save your logo as a PNG, JPG, or SVG file.

Tips and Variations:

Keep it simple and scalable for versatility.

Use a maximum of 3-4 colors to maintain visual harmony.

Ensure your logo is legible in various sizes and formats.

Create a wordmark (text-based logo) or letterform (initials) for a unique look.

Incorporate a tagline or descriptor for added context.

Experiment with different shapes, such as a circular or angular logo.

Best Practices:

Ensure your logo is memorable and distinctive.

Use a consistent color scheme across all branding materials.

Avoid clichés and overly used symbols.

Keep your logo versatile for various mediums (business cards, billboards, etc.).

Test your logo in different environments and feedback from others.

Designing a Social Media Flyer on Canva: A Step-by-Step Guide

Sign in: Log in to your Canva account or create a new one.

Search: Type "social media flyer" in the search bar and select the "Social Media Flyer" template.

Choose a template: Browse through Canva's vast template library and select a design that resonates with your brand.

Customize: Tailor the template to your liking by changing the layout, colors, fonts, and elements.

Add eye-catching visuals: Insert relevant images, graphics, or videos to grab attention.

Include essential details: Add text with key information such as date, time, location, and description.

Use attention-grabbing headlines: Craft a clear and concise headline that communicates your message.

Add a call-to-action: Encourage engagement with a prominent CTA button or link.

Experiment with fonts and colors: Select a font and color scheme that aligns with your brand and resonates with your audience.

Download and share: Save your design as a PNG, JPG, or PDF file and share it on your social media platforms.

Tips and Variations:

Use high-quality images or graphics to make your flyer stand out.

Keep your design clean and easy to read.

Use a consistent brand voice and tone.

Create a sense of urgency with limited-time offers or promotions.

Incorporate customer testimonials or reviews.

Utilize Canva's "Resize" feature to adapt your design for different social media platforms.

Experiment with different shapes, such as a circular or spiral design.

Best Practices:

Ensure your flyer is visually appealing and easy to consume.

Keep your message clear and concise.

Use a strong call-to-action to drive engagement.

Make sure your flyer is optimized for mobile devices.

Test different variations and analyze performance.

Use Canva's analytics tool to track engagement and make data-driven decisions.

Designing Instagram Reels on Canva: A Step-by-Step Guide

Sign in: Log in to your Canva account or create a new one.

Search: Type "Instagram Reel" in the search bar and select the "Instagram Reel" template.

Choose a template: Browse through Canva's vast template library and select a design that resonates with your brand.

Customize: Tailor the template to your liking by changing the layout, colors, fonts, and elements.

Add engaging visuals: Insert relevant images, graphics, or videos to capture attention.

Include text overlays: Add text with key information such as captions, quotes, or questions.

Use music and sound effects: Select a soundtrack or add sound effects to enhance the viewing experience.

Experiment with animations: Apply animations and transitions to make your Reel more dynamic.

Keep it short and sweet: Ensure your Reel is concise and within the 60-second limit.

Download and share: Save your design as a MP4 file and share it on Instagram Reels.

Tips and Variations:

Use high-quality images or graphics to make your Reel stand out.

Keep your design clean and easy to read.

Use a consistent brand voice and tone.

Create a series of Reels to tell a story or showcase a product.

Incorporate customer testimonials or reviews.

Utilize Canva's "Resize" feature to adapt your design for different social media platforms.

Experiment with different shapes, such as a circular or spiral design.

Best Practices:

Ensure your Reel is visually appealing and engaging.

Keep your message clear and concise.

Use a strong call-to-action to drive engagement.

Make sure your Reel is optimized for mobile devices.

Test different variations and analyze performance.

Use Canva's analytics tool to track engagement and make data-driven decisions.

Designing a CV or Resume on Canva: A Step-by-Step Guide

Sign in: Log in to your Canva account or create a new one.

Search: Type "CV" or "Resume" in the search bar and select the "CV" or "Resume" template.

Choose a template: Browse through Canva's vast template library and select a design that suits your style.

Customize: Tailor the template to your liking by changing the layout, colors, fonts, and elements.

Add your details: Insert your name, contact information, and professional summary.

List your experience: Add your work experience, skills, and achievements.

Education and certifications: Include your educational background and relevant certifications.

Skills and interests: Add your relevant skills, hobbies, and interests.

Achievements and awards: Include any notable achievements or awards.

Download and share: Save your design as a PDF or DOCX file and share it with potential employers.

Tips and Variations:

Use a clean and simple layout to ensure readability.

Choose a font that is professional and easy to read.

Use bullet points to break up large blocks of text.

Add relevant images or icons to enhance visual appeal.

Experiment with different colors and fonts to match your personal brand.

Use Canva's "Resize" feature to adapt your design for different formats, such as a one-page resume or a two-page CV.

Best Practices:

Ensure your CV or resume is concise and easy to scan.

Use action verbs and specific examples to describe your experience.

Tailor your CV or resume to the job you're applying for.

Proofread multiple times to ensure error-free writing.

Use a standard font size (around 10-12 points) for easy reading.

Keep your CV or resume to one or two pages, unless you have extensive experience.

Creating an eBook with Canva: A Step-by-Step Guide

Sign in: Log in to your Canva account or create a new one.

Search: Type "eBook" in the search bar and select the "eBook" template.

Choose a template: Browse through Canva's vast template library and select a design that suits your eBook's topic and style.

Customize: Tailor the template to your liking by changing the layout, colors, fonts, and elements.

Add content: Insert your eBook's text, images, and graphics.

Organize pages: Use Canva's page manager to organize your eBook's pages and sections.

Design chapters: Create visually appealing chapter headings and dividers.

Add interactive elements: Incorporate links, buttons, and other interactive elements to enhance reader engagement.

Edit and proofread: Review your eBook for errors and make necessary revisions.

Download and share: Save your eBook as a PDF or EPUB file and share it with your audience.

Tips and Variations:

Use a clear and easy-to-read font.

Choose a color scheme that resonates with your eBook's topic.

Add images and graphics to break up text and enhance visual appeal.

Use Canva's "Resize" feature to adapt your design for different formats, such as a PDF or EPUB.

Experiment with different layouts and designs to create a unique eBook.

Use Canva's collaboration tools to work with co-authors or editors.

Best Practices:

Ensure your eBook is well-organized and easy to navigate.

Use headings, subheadings, and bullet points to make your content scannable.

Optimize your eBook for mobile devices.

Use high-quality images and graphics.

Proofread multiple times to ensure error-free writing.

Use a consistent design throughout your eBook.

Creating a Website with Canva: A Step-by-Step Guide

Sign in: Log in to your Canva account or create a new one.

Search: Type "Website" in the search bar and select the "Website" template.

Choose a template: Browse through Canva's vast template library and select a design that suits your website's topic and style.

Customize: Tailor the template to your liking by changing the layout, colors, fonts, and elements.

Add pages: Create additional pages for your website, such as About, Contact, and Services.

Design pages: Use Canva's drag-and-drop editor to design each page, adding text, images, and graphics.

Add interactive elements: Incorporate links, buttons, and other interactive elements to enhance user experience.

Edit and refine: Review your website for errors and make necessary revisions.

Publish: Click "Publish" to make your website live and accessible to the public.

Share: Share your website on social media, email, or embed it on another website.

Tips and Variations:

Use a clear and easy-to-read font.

Choose a color scheme that resonates with your website's topic.

Add images and graphics to break up text and enhance visual appeal.

Use Canva's "Resize" feature to adapt your design for different devices and screen sizes.

Experiment with different layouts and designs to create a unique website.

Use Canva's collaboration tools to work with team members or clients.

Best Practices:

Ensure your website is mobile-friendly and responsive.

Use a consistent design throughout your website.

Optimize your website for search engines (SEO).

Use high-quality images and graphics.

Make sure your website is easy to navigate and user-friendly.

Regularly update your website with fresh content.

Note: Canva websites are limited to 10 pages, and e-commerce features are not available. For more advanced website features, consider using a dedicated website builder like Wix, Squarespace, or WordPress.

Creating YouTube Shorts on Canva: A Step-by-Step Guide

Sign in: Log in to your Canva account or create a new one.

Search: Type "YouTube Short" in the search bar and select the "YouTube Short" template.

Choose a template: Browse through Canva's vast template library and select a design that suits your video's topic and style.

Customize: Tailor the template to your liking by changing the layout, colors, fonts, and elements.

Add media: Insert your video clips, images, or graphics into the template.

Edit and arrange: Use Canva's drag-and-drop editor to edit and arrange your media.

Add text and effects: Incorporate text overlays, transitions, and effects to enhance your video.

Download and upload: Save your video as a MP4 file and upload it to YouTube.

Optimize for YouTube: Ensure your video meets YouTube's requirements and optimize it for the platform.

Tips and Variations:

Keep your video concise and engaging, ideally under 60 seconds.

Use high-quality media and optimize for mobile devices.

Experiment with different formats, such as vertical or square videos.

Add captions and subtitles to increase accessibility.

Use Canva's collaboration tools to work with team members or clients.

Create a series of YouTube Shorts to tell a story or showcase a product.

Best Practices:

Ensure your video is visually appealing and engaging.

Use a clear and concise narrative or message.

Optimize your video for YouTube's algorithm.

Use relevant keywords and tags.

Promote your YouTube Shorts on social media and other channels.

Analyze and adjust your video's performance using YouTube Analytics.

Designing Infographics on Canva with Creativity Tips

Start with a concept: Define the topic and message you want to convey.

Choose a template: Select a Canva infographic template that resonates with your topic.

Customize: Tailor the template to your liking by changing colors, fonts, and elements.

Add visuals: Incorporate icons, images, and graphics to break up text and enhance visual appeal.

Use data visualization: Display data and statistics in a clear and concise manner.

Keep it simple: Ensure your infographic is easy to read and understand.

Experiment with design elements: Try different shapes, colors, and typography to create a unique design.

Use storytelling techniques: Create a narrative that engages your audience.

Make it interactive: Incorporate links, animations, or other interactive elements.

Refine and iterate: Review and refine your infographic based on feedback and analytics.

Creativity Tips:

Use metaphors and analogies: Create a unique perspective on your topic.

Incorporate humor: Add a touch of humor to make your infographic more engaging.

Experiment with color: Use bold and contrasting colors to create visual interest.

Use imagery: Incorporate high-quality images that resonate with your topic.

Create a visual hierarchy: Organize your content to guide the viewer's attention.

Use typography creatively: Experiment with font sizes, styles, and colors.

Add animations and interactions: Create a dynamic and engaging infographic.

Use real-life examples: Make your infographic more relatable and tangible.

Keep it concise: Ensure your infographic is easy to scan and understand.

Have fun: Enjoy the design process and experiment with new ideas!

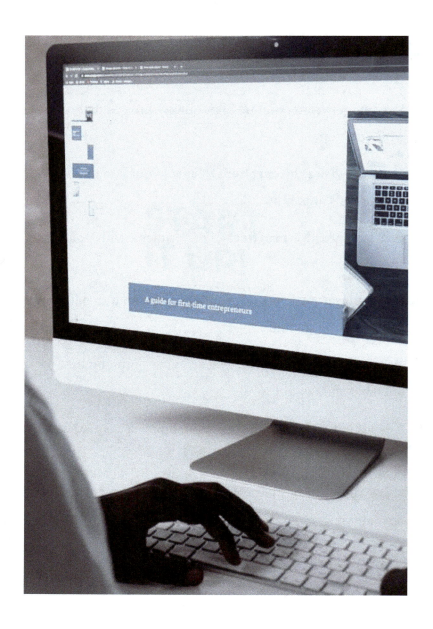

A guide for first-time entrepreneurs

CONCLUSION

Congratulations on completing the Canva Guide for Beginners! You've taken the first step towards becoming a design rockstar. Canva is an incredible tool that empowers you to create stunning visuals, even if you have no prior design experience. By mastering Canva tools and techniques, you'll be able to:

Create professional-looking designs with ease

Save time and effort with efficient design processes

Unlock your creative potential and bring your ideas to life

Collaborate seamlessly with others and communicate your vision effectively

Develop transferable skills in design principles, color theory, and visual storytelling

Boost your confidence and take on design projects with enthusiasm

Expand your design capabilities and explore new creative possibilities

Remember, practice makes perfect. Continue experimenting with Canva tools and techniques to refine your skills. Don't be afraid to try new things and make mistakes – they're an essential part of the learning process. As you start your design journey, keep in mind that Canva is a powerful tool that can help you:

Establish a strong brand identity

Create engaging social media content

Design stunning presentations and reports

Craft beautiful graphics and illustrations

Produce professional-looking documents and marketing materials

The possibilities are endless, and the Canva community is always here to support you. Share your creations, ask questions, and learn from others to continue growing as a designer.

Congratulations once again on completing the Canva Guide for Beginners! You've taken the first step towards unlocking your creative potential and becoming a design master. **Keep shining, and happy designing!**

www.ingramcontent.com/pod-product-compliance
Lightning Source LLC
LaVergne TN
LVHW052056060326
832903LV00061B/979